In 1500, there were over 1,000 different tribes in Brazil. Today, there are estimated to be 215.

'Today my people see their land invaded, their forests destroyed, their animals exterminated and their hearts lacerated by this brutal weapon that is civilisation. For the white and so-called civilised people this may seem like romanticism. But not for our people – for us it is our life.'
Kaingang woman, 1975

215 distinct peoples
53 uncontacted groups
0 lands owned by Indians

Disinherited

Indians in Brazil

CONTENTS

INTRODUCTION

'When you say that approximately six million people died in the concentration camps, the names and date of death of most are known. We indigenous peoples remember nearly six million brothers and sisters who were exterminated, and in most cases there is absolutely no information about these massacres. It was a silent and continuous extermination, which carries on even today.' Nailton Pataxó on visiting a Nazi concentration camp, 2000

Five million people, it is thought, were living in Brazil when Europeans first landed there 500 years ago. Five centuries of murder, torture, disease and exploitation have ravaged this native population. Today there are only 350,000 Brazilian Indians, and hundreds of tribes have been eradicated without trace. The fact that this was genocide is indisputable. Fifty percent of European Jews died at the hands of the Nazis; the number of Indians in Brazil has fallen by

Araweté girl

over 93% – European settlers and their Brazilian descendants have killed millions, or brought about conditions in which their death was inevitable.

Brazilian Indians today encompass a great diversity of peoples, living in tropical rainforests, grasslands, dry scrub forest and deserts. Some are now virtually indistinguishable from the mass of Brazilian poor. Many – in some cases despite centuries of intense contact – still maintain a very separate identity. Others have no contact with outsiders – Brazil is probably home to more 'uncontacted' tribes than anywhere else on earth.

Brazilian Indians are considered to be minors in law; no tribe is allowed to own land.

Such diversity is common in South America. But four things make the Brazilian Indian situation unique:

• there are a great many little-contacted, and so very vulnerable, tribes;

• Indian land ownership rights, although established in international law, are not acknowledged by the state;

• the government has an Indian affairs bureau, and plenty of money for projects to benefit Indian peoples;

• in spite of this, bar a few cases, the authorities have failed to protect Brazil's tribal peoples – some now facing their sixth century of genocide.

Brazil is the only South American country to have an active and sizeable government Indian affairs department, now the National Indian Foundation (FUNAI). The department was founded early in the last century by a compassionate army officer, and is specifically charged with protecting and assisting Indians. But it failed to prevent the demise of Indian tribes at an average rate of at least one tribe every 2 years during the course of the 20th century – at certain times, the Indian agency itself has actively contributed to the genocide.

Successive Brazilian governments have failed to put an end to this appalling human tragedy. Powerful lobbies have always been at work trying to undermine those individuals within government, and within FUNAI itself, who are sympathetic to the Indians' plight. Many politicians gain money and votes from loggers and miners, while others have their private accounts bloated by the diversion of international 'development' funds. The armed forces are continually inventing a spurious foreign threat, which they use to justify the militarisation of the border areas – where Indians live – and thus to increase their own status and power. All these find the tribal peoples of Brazil 'in the way' of their plans and ambitions. More often than not, their views have gained the

Over 40,000 goldminers invaded Yanomami land in the seven years from 1986, bringing malaria and other diseases to which the Indians had no resistance. Nearly 20% of the Yanomami were killed. This woman was among the sick airlifted out.

upper hand and any pro-Indian laws and decrees have been weakened or thrown out altogether. No sooner are the boundaries of an Indian reserve formally laid out ('demarcated') on the map than a powerful lobby tries to have it reduced or eradicated.

Over the last half century billions of dollars have flowed into the country from international agencies like the World Bank – practically all of it originating with North American and European taxpayers. The relentless work of Indian supporters has ensured that a portion of this – small, but still amounting to millions of dollars – has been allocated for the government to protect Indian land. Moreover, the Brazilian government itself undertook to complete the demarcation of all Indian lands by 1993. But one-third of the territories have still not been demarcated, and even where they have, the land is not properly protected: those who invade it

The Amazon rainforest is still being felled and burned on a colossal scale.

illegally – and often violently – do so with impunity.

If demarcation is completed and properly enforced, it does offer a modicum of protection – but even then no real security. Indian tribes remain vulnerable as long as Brazil refuses to uphold the international law which states that tribal peoples own their land, a law which, amazingly, Brazil itself formally ratified in 1965 and then promptly forgot. It is a staggering travesty of natural justice – as well as both Brazilian and international law – that in the 21st century, not one of the peoples who have inhabited Brazil for at least the last 10,000 years are deemed to own any part of it.

If this situation is compared with that in neighbouring Peru, not generally noted for its benign attitude towards Indians, then it is even clearer that Brazil has a very great deal to be ashamed of. Peru is a much poorer country (nearly twice as poor per head as Brazil), it has not received massive international aid to fund its Indian programme, it is home to more Amazonian Indians than Brazil; and yet whereas in Brazil the very best Indians can hope for is reserves – which they can merely use without actually owning any of the land – Peruvian Indians have, since 1974, enjoyed proper land titles conferring full communal ownership, in perpetuity. An average of two Peruvian Indian communities received a land title every week in the first few years after the 1974 law came into force.

It may be true that the worst excesses of Brazilian history have now ceased: the deliberate poisoning of whole Indian villages, bombing and strafing of longhouses 'in the way' of road builders, massacres of hundreds of Indians at a time – all these are things of the past and hopefully will never recur. It is also true that social scientists are no longer advising the Brazilian state to eradicate Indians, as they once did. And over the last 30 years a small but vigorous lobby of Indian supporters has grown up which permeates to senior levels of the Brazilian state and church. Most important of all, a movement of Indians themselves has taken root and given rise to dozens of Indian organisations pressing for their own rights.

Xavante at the Indian gathering in April 2000 at Coroa Vermelha to mark the 500th anniversary of the first European landing in Brazil. Riot police later opened fire on the peaceful march, bringing it to a standstill with tear gas and rubber bullets. Indians who tried to pass were beaten.

'I am proud to be part of a different people with my own land and culture. I want white people to recognise that Indians have value and I want my own people to appreciate their own culture. The Portuguese came to Brazil to conquer us, and they sent people to kill us so that they could take our land. Before, we were autonomous. In spite of everything we still have a great force. Today I am still an Indian – and I will die saying that I am Sateré Mawé.' Zenilda da Silva Vilacio, Sateré Mawé, 1998

Yet it remains the case that Indians are still being killed and virtually no one is ever successfully prosecuted for it. Today Indian children as young as nine are committing suicide in despair at their lack of land and a future. And a large number of Indians are still succumbing to fatal diseases which they catch as a direct result of the invasion of their lands: a recent malaria epidemic, sparked by miners, killed nearly 20% of the Yanomami in only seven years.

Tribes contacted recently, and who are being contacted now, still risk annihilation. If they survive at all, they face decimation and enormous suffering, just as they would have done in past centuries. The only long-term solution – the only guarantee of security for Brazil's Indian peoples – is for the Brazilian government to honour international law and finally recognise Indian land ownership. Its refusal to do so is a clear demonstration of the most extreme institutional racism; but it is so ingrained in Brazilian attitudes that even many Indian supporters fear that if the question is raised it will provoke strong anti-Indian feeling in the corridors of power.

This book does not attempt a comprehensive account of Brazil's Indian peoples. It focuses on a few specific tribes, and largely on the least contacted peoples, the most vulnerable of all Brazil's Indians, illustrating their predicament by describing particular cases. It argues that they face genocide – no longer with intent perhaps, but genocide nonetheless – in the same way that tribes have done in Brazil since the first Europeans arrived there five centuries ago. Such a heinous crime can never be merely an 'internal' matter for Brazil, it is a crime against humanity – that is, against all of us – and so becomes the business and responsibility of everyone.

VENEZUELA GUYANA FRENCH GUIANA

COLOMBIA SURINAME

Yanomami

Boa Vista Waiãpi

Makuxi
Wapixana Belém
Ingarikó Arara
Taurepang Araweté

Tukano Manaus Sateré Mawé

PERU

Tikuna Amazonia

Matis
Korubo

Kayapó
Panará
Cinta Larga Kayabí Tapayúna
Oro Uim Enawene Nawe
Kanoê Xingu Park
Nambiquara Xavante
Pareci Bororo
Irantxe
Umutima BOLIVIA

Savannah

Guarani

PARAGUAY

CHILE

ARGENTINA

Kaingang

URUGUAY

PACIFIC

6   Map

Map

showing the tribes featured in this book

Ka'apor
Awá

Arid north-east

Avá
Canoeiro
Xacriabá
Brasília

Pataxó Hã Hã Hãe
Maxakali
Cabrália – where the
Portugese first landed

Tupinikim

Rio de Janeiro
São Paulo

ATLANTIC

215 tribes in all

11% of Brazil
designated
Indian land
Territories range from
9.4 million hectares
for the Yanomami to
9 hectares for 400
Guarani in Campestre.

0% of land in Brazil
owned by tribal
peoples

Map   7

In 1500, there were around five million Brazilian Indians. Today, there are 350,000.

The longest genocide

Before 1500

It is not known for certain how the first peoples in Brazil arrived in their land. The accepted explanation is that 30,000–40,000 years ago hunter gatherer tribes crossed the strip of land which then linked Asia to Alaska, and that their descendants gradually spread south through the continents, reaching Brazil by about 10,000 BC. But some believe that recently discovered rock paintings and the remains of settlements in the arid interior of Brazil date back further than this theory can explain, even to as much as 50,000 years ago. In light of this, it has been suggested that a number of tribes made their way to South America much earlier, perhaps by sea.

Umutima shaman. A measles epidemic killed the last 75 members of his village in 1969, after only two generations of contact with white people.

Certainly, by the time the Europeans arrived in Brazil, it was home to at least 1,000 tribes, and estimates of the population place it at between five and six million. There was a great diversity of peoples, ranging from agricultural societies settled in towns in the Amazon flood plains, possessors of a rich material culture who could mobilise large, powerful armies, to hunter gatherer peoples living in the uplands or forest away from the rivers – these peoples were probably egalitarian and largely nomadic societies, living in small mobile groups similar to modern hunter gatherers.

1500-1900

The first encounter with Europeans took place on 22 April 1500 in the land of the Tupinikim Indians, who then numbered tens of thousands and of whom there are today less than 1,000. The exchange of a hat for a feather headdress was to mark

the beginning of an invasion which would soon wipe out millions. The early contact was reasonably friendly, characterised by trading and European fascination with the 'exotic' Indians, some of whom were taken to Europe to be paraded as curiosities. Many European writers and philosophers, such as Montaigne, and later Rousseau, were inspired by the apparent freedom and honesty of the Indians: their writings made popular the (still current) notion of the 'noble savage'.

But the attitudes of Europeans in Brazil were increasingly more hostile. The Indian-settler relationship had its terms dictated by the more powerful weapons of the Europeans, and their desire to amass material wealth – an ambition bewildering for many of the indigenous peoples they encountered. As the Portuguese and other European arrivals began their plunder of this newly encountered land, thousands of Indians were enslaved and forced to work for European masters. Whole tribes were wiped out by the horrors of slavery, and thousands of individuals by exposure to new diseases to which they had no immunity. By the 17th century there were so few Indians left on the coast that slaves from Africa were imported to work in the sugar plantations. Although slavery of Indians was finally abolished in 1755 and of black people in 1888, the practice continued openly right up until the end of the 19th century, perpetuated

Engraving of Botocudo Indian family, c.1835. Renowned for resisting military attacks, the Botocudo rose up against the Capuchin missionaries who had forced them to live in settled villages and had taken their children away. Many Indians were killed when the army was called in, and a further 400 died from a subsequent measles epidemic.

'The injustices and tyrannies practised on the Indians in these lands exceed by far those done in Africa. In the space of 40 years there were destroyed along this coast and in the interior more than 2 million Indians and more than 500 Indian settlements as large as cities and no punishments have been given for this.' Antonio Vieira, Jesuit priest, 1657

'The work [on the sugar plantations] is insufferable. Many slaves die... the owners commit so many sins.'

Fernão Cardim, Jesuit priest, 1584

by the 'rubber barons', who, during the 'rubber boom' of the late 19th and early 20th centuries, ruthlessly exploited the Amazon and its inhabitants. 'Debt bondage', a less explicit form of slavery, was common up to the 1970s, and even today there are cases of Indians being held in debt bondage or wage slavery – like the Guarani and Xacriabá Indian plantation workers.

In 1609, King Philip II of Portugal proclaimed the 'full freedom' of Indians but also decreed that they were 'legal minors' – this refusal to recognise Indians legally as adults, and the denial of all the rights that such recognition entails, continues even today. For hundreds of years they were therefore 'entrusted' to different authorities –

firstly missionaries, then colonial government officials – whose attempts to round up, assimilate and convert or exploit these native peoples led only to despair and death. Thousands were wiped out by epidemics, while many others were worn out by labour.

Throughout this history, many of the Indians of Brazil have resisted exploitation and attack, fighting to defend their lands and rights, or evading those who would oppress them. Some Indian peoples fought European forces in large-scale battles, often winning and holding off the invaders for a time; other tribes resisted most successfully by employing guerrilla tactics. But in the end, the sheer numbers of the colonists, and the weapons available to them, always allowed them to prevail – if the Indians had not already been defeated by disease.

1900

The Indians did eventually have some champions among the administration. Cândido Mariano da Silva Rondon was the founder and first head of the government's Indian Protection Service (SPI), formed in 1910. Himself the great-grandson of a Bororo Indian, his intentions towards them were undoubtedly good. Yet the organisation he headed, with its aim of assimilating Indians into 'mainstream' society, was ultimately disastrous for them. As resources were cut, and the idealists, including Rondon himself, were succeeded by incompetent, unsympathetic and sometimes corrupt bureaucrats, abuses of Indians went unchecked. SPI's failure to provide medical assistance to vulnerable tribes and to secure adequate protection for Indian land led to many deaths.

1940s – 1960s

Although in the late 1940s and early 1950s the SPI had good periods, a more effective pro-Indian movement was fostered by the work of the Villas Bôas brothers. They felt both admiration and respect for the Indian peoples they encountered, but had an approach directed more at protection than trying to secure rights or self-determination. In the 1950s, they established the Xingu Park, at the time regarded as a radical project and one to be emulated. This Indian 'safe haven' became home to 16 tribes, some of which traded their

INDIAN NAMES

Despite the domination of Brazilian society by the descendants of the Portuguese and other European settlers, Indian names are found everywhere. Many mountains, rivers and places – such as Guanabara Bay in Rio de Janeiro – have Indian names. Manaus, the capital of Amazonas state, is named after the extinct Manoa tribe which once lived there. The name of the mighty Iguaçu Falls means 'big waters', and the Maracanã football stadium in Rio takes its name from a Tupi-Guarani word which means 'large rattle' and is also the name of a type of parrot.

Tupi, one of the main Indian language groups in Brazil, has had an important and lasting influence on Brazilian language and terminology. The first Europeans adapted Tupi-Guarani to communicate with the Tupi speaking tribes. The adapted language spread throughout Brazil and became known as *lingua geral* – it is still spoken by some people in the Amazon today.

Many animals, birds and fish have Indian names – 'cayman' is the Carib word for alligator. 'Hammock' is also a Carib word, and 'tapioca' is a Tupi word meaning 'squeezed out dregs'.

THE CINTA LARGA MASSACRE

The people known as the 'Cinta Larga' suffered many vicious and gruesome attacks at the hands of rubber tappers between the 1920s and the 1960s. One famous incident, the 1963 'massacre of the 11th parallel', took place in the headwaters of the Aripuanã river where the firm of Arruda, Junqueira & Co was collecting rubber. The head of the company, Antonio Mascarenhas Junqueira, planned the massacre, deeming the Cinta Larga to be in the way of his commercial activities: 'These Indians are parasites, they are shameful. It's time to finish them off, it's time to eliminate these pests. Let's liquidate these vagabonds.'

He hired a small plane, from which sticks of dynamite were hurled into a Cinta Larga village below. Later, some of the killers returned on foot to finish off the survivors – finding a woman breastfeeding her child, they shot the baby's head off, and then hung her upside down and sliced her in half. The judge at the trial of one of the accused said, 'We have never listened to a case where there was so much violence, so much ignominy, egoism and savagery and so little appreciation of human life.'

In 1975 one of the perpetrators, José Duarte de Prado, was sentenced to 10 years imprisonment, but was pardoned later that year. He declared during the trial, 'It's good to kill Indians – they are lazy and treacherous.'

ancestral lands outside the park for security and health inside. It is easy now to criticise the paternalism of such a scheme, in which the Indians were given no choice, but at the time there were few prepared to stand up for Brazil's tribal peoples – and the Villas Bôas brothers did so at considerable personal risk. They saw their policy of contacting and relocating threatened tribes as often the

Kayapó Indians. In 1989 they protested at Altamira against government proposals to build hydroelectric dams along the Xingu river. Their protest aroused worldwide support and the project was shelved. Had it gone ahead, the dam would have flooded much of their territory.

only alternative to integration, to which they were totally opposed: 'To integrate, pacify and acculturate are absurd expressions, perhaps even criminal. Integration has been a disastrous policy.'

In 1967 the true extent of the 'criminal' actions against the native population of Brazil was exposed, with the completion of the Figueiredo report into the treatment of Brazilian Indians. The 5,000 page document revealed a catalogue of atrocities. It documented mass murder, torture and bacteriological warfare, reported slavery, sexual abuse, theft and neglect – mostly during just the previous seven years. It was reported that groups

'They faced dogs, chains, Winchesters, machine guns, napalm, arsenic, clothes contaminated with smallpox, false certificates, removal, deportations, highways, fences, fires, weeds, cattle, the decrees of law and the denial of facts.'

Darcy Ribeiro, Brazilian anthropologist and senator, 1981

of Pataxó Indians had been deliberately infected with smallpox; the Tapayúna (Beiços de Pau) were poisoned with arsenic and ant killer; the Maxacali were given alcohol by landowners whose gunmen then shot them down while they were drunk. The author of the report likened the suffering of the Indians to that experienced in Nazi concentration camps, and concluded that 80 tribes had disappeared completely. The SPI's own criminal neglect was responsible for much of the suffering, and for the loss of whole tribes.

The judicial enquiry launched in the wake of the report led to 134 government officials being charged with over 1,000 crimes – 38 were dismissed. No-one ever went to prison for these atrocities. The report was never made public – few people outside the government even saw it, and several years after publication it was burned in a mysterious fire in government offices. But in Brazil it had already caused a public outcry which had repercussions around the world. A British newspaper, the Sunday Times, sent writer Norman Lewis to investigate. His article, 'Genocide', shocked the public and led to the founding of Survival International in 1969. In the next three years, missions by the Red Cross, Survival International and the Aborigines Protection Society visited dozens of tribes, and the publication of their findings brought the Brazilian Indian situation to international attention.

Matis woman and child.

Indians like these Tehuka
terminated in the jungles
Brazilian Ministry of the I
a commission set up to inv
against the Indian popula
group of nations at the U.

GENOCIDE

'From fire and sword to arsenic and bullets – civilisation has sent six million Indians to extinction.' Sunday Times, 1969. This article by Norman Lewis led to the founding of Survival International soon afterwards.

The discredited SPI was replaced in 1967 with FUNAI (National Indian Foundation), which still today has responsibility for Indian affairs. Chronically underfunded and unnecessarily bureaucratic, it has often been weakened – or even controlled – by anti-Indian politicians and officials. One of its former presidents described Indians as 'ethnic cysts' which 'Brazil will not tolerate within its borders'; others, like Romero Jucá, were accused of the illegal sales of lucrative logging contracts on Indian lands.

EMANCIPATION

In 1981, the Brazilian government came up with a new plan to strip Indian tribes of their land. In just 10 days, the government Indian department produced criteria of 'Indianness', contained in a report which stated that Indians had 'undesirable biological, psychic and cultural characteristics'.

The criteria for 'Indianness' were based on whether an individual wore clothes and spoke the national language. Those judged to be 'Indian' were to continue to be deprived of many social and political rights. But those who were not, including any who spoke Portuguese, were to be 'emancipated' – no longer considered minors in law, but with the loss of all rights to live on or use Indian land.

Protest was swift. Daniel Cabixi, a Pareci Indian, declared that 'this emancipation is a lethal weapon which will simply take from us all chance and every weapon which we have to protest against the infringement of our rights.' A Brazilian bishop described the emancipation project as 'a sophisticated act of genocide'.

Survival mounted an international campaign. In the face of protests in Brazil and abroad the government backed down.

PRISONS

FUNAI established its own prison – secret for many years – which was described by one former employee as a 'concentration camp'. Rebel Indians who opposed FUNAI were sent there and subjected to forced labour. But it never had a large number of inmates, and collapsed after some years.

The prison was also used to train young men for the 'Indian Guard' – a government-run force first established by the Indian Protection Service, whose members, imbued with 'military discipline', were intended to return to Indian villages and create a reign of terror. After eight years of protest the Indian Guard was dissolved in 1974.

1970s – 1990s

FUNAI's explicit aim was to 'integrate' Indians – regardless of their own wishes. Meanwhile the Amazon was being opened up by massive road-building and 'development' schemes, for which the motivation was partly economic, and partly political: overcrowding in north-east and south Brazil was breeding discontent with the government, which it misguidedly attempted to diffuse by relocating settlers in the Amazon. The army also demanded access to the Amazonian border areas, to defend against perceived threats from Brazil's less powerful neighbours. The influx of settlers brought more disease, and Indians were again being driven off their lands, this time to make way for dams, mines, roads and cattle ranches.

During the 1970s, some Indian peoples, increasingly aware that the violence and discrimination they suffered were experienced by others throughout the country, began to unite to demand their rights. The first national Indian assembly was held in 1977, and the first Brazilian Indian organisation, the Union of Indian Nations (UNI), was formed in 1980. Predictably, the government said it would not be supported, or even permitted – 'Indians do not have full civil rights: such an entity would be illegal, as the Indians are considered minors.' But the Indian rights movement refused to be silenced. Today over 100 Indian organisations, all unique, operate locally and nationally, and new ones are being formed all the time. They vary greatly in size and level of organisation. Most of those in Amazonia are members of the coordinating body COIAB.

In addition, there are many non-Indian support organisations in Brazil. Some were founded by missionaries, others by anthropologists or other Indian experts. The oldest are the Indian Missionary Council (CIMI), started by pro-Indian Roman Catholic missionaries, and the Pro-Yanomami Commission (CCPY), which was founded by Claudia Andujar and others and which was instrumental in getting Yanomami land recognised in 1992. Other important pro-Indian organisations today include the Socio-Environmental Institute (ISA), the Indigenous Advocacy Centre (CTI), the Pro-Indian Commission (CPI-SP), and Operation Native Amazon (OPAN).

2000 – sixth century of genocide

Yet violence and abuse against Indians continue. In recent years, for example, Pataxó Hã Hã Hãe have been forcibly sterilised, Tikuna at a meeting massacred by loggers, and uncontacted Indians shot and mutilated. Today's Indian peoples are fighting back, and have many dedicated supporters – but they still suffer attacks and persecution from settlers and corporate entities who want their land at any price; neglect from a government which still regards them as minors and refuses to allow Indian land ownership; and stereotyping from the outside world, to whom they are exotic showpieces, ecological heroes or backward primitives.

Uncontacted

There are currently estimated to be at least 70 uncontacted peoples in the world. The vast majority of them – probably more than 50 – are in Brazil. These uncontacted Brazilian tribes range in size from those such as the Akuntsu and Kanoê, who number only a few dozen, to the Korubo and Awá, of whom there are thought to be 100-200.

The reality of what it means to be 'uncontacted' in the 21st century is rather complicated. Some peoples may indeed never have had contact with white or black Brazilians, but they would certainly, at least in the past, have known neighbouring tribes. And a number would also have had contact with settlers – even if hundreds of years

ago. Some of the uncontacted 'peoples' are in fact small groups of a tribe, other members of which now live in contact with outsiders, often in government-established 'contact posts'. Staying out of contact is not easy – retreating into remoter zones is a deliberate decision, made to evade attacks by new diseases, armed white men, loggers, slave raiders or missionaries.

Even when tribes remain 'hidden' – sometimes for centuries – they will regularly spy on others and even take some of their goods when they can. They would equally readily resort to killing people, if need be: to a tribe whose only

A woman from the only contacted group of Korubo. Her people have suffered many violent attacks over recent years and their land is increasingly threatened by loggers. The vast majority of the Korubo live uncontacted in the Javari valley.

There are at least 50 uncontacted tribes in Brazil – more than anywhere else.

A Korubo Indian who has just been contacted looks through the camera lens at a Matis member of the contact mission. Since contact, these Korubo have remained in the forest and thus protected themselves from disease.

knowledge of outsiders comes from stories of murderous men with powerful weapons, the approach of a white man will justifiably appear a mortal threat. Yet uncontacted tribes will usually be friendly to those who approach them peacefully – aggression is much more likely to come from white outsiders.

Most of Brazil's uncontacted peoples live in the Amazon rainforest, and practise a semi-nomadic or nomadic lifestyle, continually moving on and thus avoiding contact. But for many this is

not in fact their 'traditional' way of life: the Awá, for instance, were once settled agriculturalists, whose adoption of a life of flight was to escape the constant attacks by outsiders.

All the uncontacted peoples have sophisticated and detailed knowledge of the natural environment, as they must if they are to survive – often their lands are the less appealing, less fertile areas, where settlers are less likely to follow them, but where it also takes skill to survive.

Matis Indian preparing a blowgun dart by wrapping cotton at one end to act as a flight. Blowguns, which tend to be nearly three metres long, are very accurate weapons, used to hunt birds and monkeys.

POISONS

Throughout South America, tribes have developed the use of naturally occurring poisons as an important hunting tool. Curare poison, for instance, can be made from several plants. Bark is boiled up and smeared over the the tip of an arrow or dart. These poisons act as a powerful muscle relaxant, paralysing the prey, but have no effect when the meat is eaten. And it is not only plants that provide poison – some species of frog are also used.

In the Amazon more than 30 different plants and lianas (woody vines) are used as fish poisons. They are beaten and pulverised, and the resulting pulp placed in a stream. The poisons stun the fish – which then rise to the surface and are easily caught in baskets – but again leave them fully edible, as the poisons are not absorbed. Any fish not caught soon recover and swim away.

FUNAI, the government Indian affairs department, set up a unit for uncontacted Indians in 1988. Its policy now is to make contact with such peoples only if there are serious threats to them – as in the case of the Korubo community which was under threat from loggers and was contacted in the western Amazon in 1996. In line with this policy, FUNAI has demarcated an area, Massacó, without any contact with the tribe inhabiting it. Sydney Possuelo of FUNAI described this demarcation as 'a landmark… This is the first Indian territory in Brazil to be demarcated without our knowing anything about the group – we don't know their name, their language or how many there are. It is not important to know them or study them, what is important is to guarantee their survival.'

But Brazil's uncontacted peoples are still its most vulnerable – they are at risk from invasion and all the dangers of contact, and, while they have knowledge of how to survive in the forest or bush, they know little of how to defend their rights against powerful interests. Survival is campaigning for the land ownership rights of all uncontacted peoples in Brazil to be recognised and protected as a matter of urgency.

An Awá hunting group with their catch of tortoises, agouti and birds.

110 tribal languages in Brazil have less than 400 speakers each.

On the run

THE AWÁ

The Awá (called Guajá by other Indians and non-Indian Brazilians) are one of Brazil's few nomadic hunter gatherer tribes. No-one knows how many of them there are: 250 who have been contacted now live in four Indian territories, including one right beside the Carajás railway, and FUNAI, the government Indian department, estimates that there are up to 100 living uncontacted as nomads. Reports are regularly received of Awá groups sighted near towns or raiding plantations for food. Their home is in the devastated forests of the eastern Amazon, and is increasingly threatened by industrial 'development' projects.

There is strong evidence that the Awá are one of those tribal peoples who were once settled horticulturalists, but who were forced to abandon this for a

Rapatia and Hoyeera, an Awá couple, survived a massacre with their baby – the rest of their group was killed. This picture was taken two days after they were contacted by a government team in 1992.

nomadic way of life – in their case in around 1800 – because of the invasions of white settlers and the diseases they brought. Many Awá were lost to such disease and to violence at the hands of these settlers. They fragmented into small groups of 20-30 people which made it easier to keep on the run – a nomadic life offered them the best chance of survival in the face of such threats. Those who are still nomadic are highly mobile, travelling from camp to camp carrying slow-burning embers to make fires.

The persecution they have faced over the last 50 years has been even worse than that which forced them into nomadism in the first place. Many groups have suffered systematic extermination at the hands of ranchers and settlers. In 1979, for example, seven uncontacted Awá died of poisoning when farmers left out a 'gift' of flour laced with ant killer. Many Awá in the Alto Turiaçu, first contacted by a government contact team

'The destruction of the Indians of the Americas was, far and away, the most massive act of genocide in the history of the world.'
David E Stannard, historian, 1992

in the early 1970s, died from a flu epidemic introduced by the team.

Most of those Awá who have been contacted – and many who have not – are the survivors of brutal massacres, which have left them mentally and physically scarred. One such survivor is Karapiru, whose incredible story illustrates the resilience of the Awá people. In 1988, in a town in west Bahia, locals began to report that their animals were being hit with arrows. Some time later, only a couple of miles outside the town, a farmer saw a lone Indian walking in the scrub, carrying arrows, a machete, several water containers and a piece of smoked pork. The farmer followed the Indian, who, realising he was being watched, left his belongings on the ground, one by one. They greeted each other and the Indian followed the farmer back to the village, where he stayed with a local family whom he helped to cut wood and to feed the pigs.

As news spread of the 'unknown' Indian, intrigued anthropologists came to visit him. They realised his language was of the Tupi language group, and thought he might be an Avá Canoeiro – but when FUNAI took him to the capital and introduced him to some members of that tribe, they could not communicate.

FUNAI then arranged for a young Awá man to come to Brasilia – not only could the Indians speak to each other, but Karapiru recognised the young man brought by FUNAI as his own son, Tiramucum, whom he thought had been killed 13 years previously.

They had been separated in about 1975 when Karapiru and his family had been attacked by ranchers. The boy, Tiramucum, was wounded by the attackers, who later took him to their home. Some years lapsed before FUNAI brought him to a post they had established to contact the Awá. Karapiru and his daughter, Korain, also survived the attack and fled for their lives. Korain died from her wounds soon afterwards, and for 12 years Karapiru lived on his own, silently watching but avoiding whites. He would sleep in tree tops and talk and hum to himself. During his lonely exile, he walked nearly 400 miles to Bahia.

In 1992 there was more good news: Karapiru was reunited with his brother who had also just been contacted by FUNAI. Karapiru now lives with his new wife, Manimi, and their daughter, Makriankwa, in the Awá village of Tiracambú.

The Awá people are still under threat, and are vulnerable to the sort of attack that Karapiru's family suffered. The massive Carajás industrial project received funding from the World Bank and European Union for the building of dams, railways, roads and mines. The Awá have seen industrial development on a huge scale on their lands, and with it roads, bringing in wave after wave of colonists, loggers and miners. Despite agreeing to demarcate all Indian lands in the area as a condition of the 1982 World Bank loan, the authorities have done nothing to protect the uncontacted Awá. More than ever, the remaining, traumatised Awá need their land if they are to survive.

KARAPIRU'S STORY

as told to Survival, 2000

'At the time of the massacre, I was the only survivor of the family – I hid in the forest, and escaped from the white people. They killed my mother, my brothers and sisters and my wife. I lived, always managing to escape from the ranchers. I walked a long, long way, always hiding in the forest. I was very hungry and it was very hard to survive. I ate small birds; later, when I travelled far from the place where the massacre happened, I began to take animals from the white people here or there, but I would then always flee. I ate honey. I found a machete, and I would always carry that with me – it was a weapon and also helped me get the honey.

'When I was shot during the massacre, I suffered a great deal because I couldn't put any medicine on my back. I couldn't see the wound: it was amazing that I escaped – it was through the Tupã [spirit]. I spent days wandering around in pain, with the lead shot in my back, bleeding. I don't know how it didn't get full of insects. But I managed to escape from the whites.

'I spent a long time in the forest, hungry and being chased by ranchers. I was always running away, on my own. I had no family to help me, to talk to. So I went deeper and deeper into the forest. Today I couldn't tell you where I went. It was very sad and there are times when I don't like to remember all that happened to me, that time I spent in the forest. I feel good here with the other Awá. And I have found my son after many years.

'I hope when my daughter grows up she won't face any of the difficulties I've had. I hope everything will be better for her. I hope the same things that happened to me won't happen to her. I hope she will grow up very healthy. I hope it won't be like in my time.'

First contact

Contact is the greatest danger for an isolated tribe. It is (and long has been) common for a tribe's population to plummet by 50% or more after encountering non-Indians. For instance, the Mëbêngôkre (a group of Kayapó) were reduced from 350 to 85 in the first six months after contact in 1936. Eighty percent of the Panará were wiped out within 10 years of first contact in the early 1970s. The Kabixi and Marawá are among many who have been destroyed completely. There are countless similar stories, some not even known – often a tribe has been wiped out before its story is recorded or even its name established.

One important factor in these deaths is the exposure to new diseases which contact brings: malaria, probably not present in the Americas before the European arrival and still not affecting some remote areas, is a major killer; so are simple infections like flu, to which the Indians have no natural immunity. With the onset of these illnesses – new and unknown to the tribe's own healers and for which appropriate medicines are not available to them – the sick cannot hunt or collect crops, and so hunger and further weakness inevitably follow. Alongside disease comes the psychological shock of encountering a people who seem determined to take over one's land, who have technology and weapons of undreamt-of force, and – perhaps most importantly – are so populous as to seem without number.

Throughout most of the 20th century – prompted by a racist belief that Indians were 'primitive' and that contact would be 'good for them' whatever their own wishes – Brazil, alone among

Gifts left out by a government contact team to attract a group of Panará. Knives are especially prized by uncontacted Indians as they far more effective than stone tools.

GUARANÁ

Guaraná is a drink which Indians have made for hundreds, if not thousands, of years by roasting and grinding the guaraná nut. It is a natural stimulant, used as such especially for hunting, with a higher caffeine content than coffee or tea. It is important for rituals, and is used to cure headaches and fever.

White people were introduced to guaraná in 1669, when they first met the Sateré Mawé. It has become a hugely popular fizzy drink in Brazil, as common as coca cola, and the trade is still extremely important to the Sateré Mawé. Today 300 tons of guaraná are produced annually in the Amazon in stick, powder or liquid form.

Amazonian countries, mounted special contact expeditions. In these, which sometimes lasted several years, government experts and Indian trackers would move into the territory of an uncontacted tribe, and put out 'presents' such as knives and cooking pots. The uncontacted Indians would take the gifts, and a trusting relationship would be built up, the whites leaving more presents and the Indians reciprocating with their own. Once friendly contact was established, the flow of presents would cease. The failure of contact teams to provide medical backup to the vulnerable Indians – despite the risks being known – left them ravaged by disease. At this point the tribe would often be moved out of the way of 'development'.

Bina is half Matis and half Korubo, from the Javari valley near the Peruvian border. He encountered a government contact expedition as a boy, and told his story to Survival in 1996.

'The first thing I remember was the plane above our village. It dropped machetes,

axes and blankets. Then it came back another day and dropped more things. I remember we were making poison for hunting. The plane disappeared and I had no idea who it was. Then FUNAI [the government Indian department] arrived. They came up our trail and left us things, they hung up knives and pans. At first we were very frightened of the whites because they always want to kill us. So I ran into the forest. Later we went down to the FUNAI camp and that was our first contact. They gave us axes and machetes and we also took two dogs. Then we went back to our village and told everyone about it. We kept going back for more and lots of women went too. I tried to talk with the whites but they didn't understand. But we caught illnesses in their camp and then everyone rushed into the forest... We got pneumonia. A lot of people died. Disease hit everyone and now we don't have shamans any more.'

Often the villages of uncontacted Indians are first sighted from the air. It took years to locate this Panará village in the early 1970s.

'One day we saw a beetle flying over the top of our house. It was a very big beetle carrying a lot of people. But they were not like us, they were a different people. It was a very big beetle which had arrived to dominate us.'

Orlando Makuxi, 1996

'It is necessary to finish with Indians by the year 2000.'

Hélio Jaguaribe, ex-minister, 1994

DAVI YANOMAMI IN ENGLAND

In 1989, Survival was awarded the prestigious Right Livelihood Award, known as the 'alternative Nobel prize'. Survival asked a Yanomami spokesman, Davi, to receive the award on its behalf. Davi's visit to Europe, his first outside Brazil, received massive press attention and catapulted the campaign for a protected Yanomami area into the international arena. This was a decisive factor in the government's final agreement to a Yanomami park three years later. Davi Yanomami later said of England:

'I remember how strange it all was – a big city, such noise and so many big buildings. The forest was small and sparse and cut back. So many people! Also the noise of the train, and cars. I was sad because it was such a polluted place.

'I was frightened in England – so much noise and activity; conflicts, thieves. I thought the land was beautiful, but not the buildings. So many people living all on top of one another 1-2-3-4-5 storeys, they were like wasps in a wasps' nest! The people are so different. I thought many places were beautiful, despite the pollution and the cold – such cold! A cold place where the whites began.'

The Matis contact happened in 1978 and rapidly killed over half of them. They stopped practising their ceremonies and, like many Indians suffering from the trauma of first contact, stopped having children. By 1983, only 87 had survived.

From the 1970s, after witnessing many such tragedies and the deaths of so many Indians who had come to trust them, some of Brazil's best experts refused to continue with contact expeditions, saying they had had their fill of 'digging graves' for those they had befriended. The policy is now practised only where Indians are already in danger.

A Panará village photographed by the Villas Bôas team when they flew over the area as part of their attempt to contact the Indians in the early 1970s.

Commonly the populations of tribes which do survive contact begin to grow again after 20-30 years. A few peoples contacted in the last couple of generations are now quite vigorous societies (though they are not without many problems). These recoveries are encouraging and impressive – but should not mask the appalling suffering of the thousands of Indians whose tribes have been, and are being today, decimated and even annihilated by 'civilisation'.

Dangerous contact is still happening in many parts of Brazil. But if – as Survival is urging – little-contacted peoples have their land properly protected, best of all by recognising their ownership of it, it would give them a chance of survival.

Homeward bound

THE PANARÁ

The tale of the Panará is a classic example of a story repeated countless times in South America: a remote tribe hemmed into an ever smaller area by the colonisation of their land, the inevitable contact with white people, and the death of most of the tribe from disease. This time, though, there was an unexpected and significant twist in the tale.

Throughout the 1960s there were rumours of a tribe of giant, secretive Indians living in central Brazil. The Kayapó, a neighbouring tribe, called them 'Kren Akrore' ('short-haired people') whilst to the Kayabi Indians to the west they were the 'Ipeuí' or 'small trap people', since anyone who tried to follow them after a raid ran the risk of impaling themselves on pointed sticks buried beneath leaves.

One of the first Panará to encounter the contact team, led by the Villas Bôas brothers, in 1973. The photograph was taken as he appeared on the river bank.

By the 1970s there were between 350 and 400 Panará (as they call themselves) living in five villages – many of them had already been killed by the Kayapó, who had in their turn been pushed onto Panará land by white colonisation. These 'giants' decorated their bodies with symmetrical scars and cultivated crops in enormous gardens which they laid out in complex geometric designs. Their villages had large central men's and boys' houses, which were surrounded by smaller dwellings. They slept on banana leaves and used earth mounds as pillows. Food was usually baked in banana leaves between hot stones.

By 1972, road-building crews had bulldozed their way through Panará territory – waves of disease followed the road crews, killing yet more of the Panará. Peaceful contact was finally made by Indian expert Claudio

AMAZONS

Many fantastic stories have been told about Brazil and its peoples over the centuries. One of the earliest was about a tribe of fierce women warriors, whom 16th century Spanish travellers claimed to have heard stories of, and even seen: 'These women are very white and tall, with very long hair braided and wound about their heads. They are very robust, and go naked with their private parts covered, with their bows and arrows in their hands, doing as much fighting as ten Indian men' (Friar Gaspar de Carvajal, 1542). The Europeans named them 'Amazons' after the women warriors of Greek mythology.

It is probable that the Spaniards simply mistook long haired men, or men wearing grass skirts (like the Yagua) for women. But whether fantasy or not, the 'Amazons' have been immortalised in the name of the mighty river.

Villas Bôas in 1973: unsurprisingly, the 'giants' turned out to be no taller than average.

In the following five months, 40 Indians died of diseases like flu and chicken pox, which were new to them. The road-builders gave them alcohol and used the women for sex. Akè, a Panará leader, recalls this tragic time, 'We were in the village and everybody began to die. Some people went into the forest and more died there. We were ill and weak, so we couldn't even bury our dead. They just lay rotting on the ground. The vultures ate everything.'

The Villas Bôas brothers decided that the only way to save the Panará was to transfer them to the newly-created Indian 'safe haven' of the Xingu Park. In a letter to Survival, Orlando Villas Bôas explained why. 'In principle we are opposed to dislodging contacted Indians outside their area of adaptation. Clearly

all their world and customs are there... In the case of the Kren Akrore things are different. Their area is violently threatened. So long as they live in their traditional area they will always be close to nuclei of settlements or the opened road and exposed to indiscriminate contact. A road close by invites the Indians' curiosity towards improvident settlers, who are indifferent to the harm they bring. We therefore conclude that the only salvation would be the withdrawal of the Indians. Withdrawal to a place where for some time – which God may permit will be a long time – they can remain protected from encroachment by invaders.'

One hundred and eighty six Indians died between 1973 and 1975, and the survivors were airlifted into the Xingu Park, where yet more died. Soon only 69 Panará were left: more than four-fifths of the tribe had been killed in eight years.

But the Panará never adapted to their new home, moving seven times in the Xingu Park. The land was no good for their agriculture, hunting was poor and there were some conflicts with other tribes in the park. Panará ceremonies were no longer performed, and the boys' house was no longer built – the women had stopped having children.

And here one might have expected the story would end. Yet the Panará had an intense longing to return to their home, and never gave up hope that they might one day go back. In 1991, six Panará went back to their territory, now virtually destroyed by miners and ranchers. Seeing the devastation galvanised Akè and his friends into fighting back and claiming compensation. 'The old man [Brazilian authorities] will have to listen to me. Our land has been razed. Our land has been eaten… The good land has gone, all the fruit trees have gone. The old man will have to pay me.'

Flying over their land, the Panará identified an area in the headwaters

of the Iriri river which was still not destroyed. They decided to give up their rights to the rest of their land in return for the legal recognition of this area. In August 1994, they started to build a village there, and during the next two years the Panará gradually moved back. Finally, in 1996, the Minister of Justice signed a decree recognising the 495,000 hectares as Panará land – though not giving them ownership of it. After two decades in exile, the Panará had returned to their homeland.

And there was more. The Brazilian Socio-Environmental Institute (ISA) decided to sue the government for the appalling conditions inflicted upon the Panará. On 22 October 1997, a judge found the Brazilian state guilty of 'causing death and cultural harm' to the Panará Indians – a landmark judgment which would have been unthinkable even ten years before. Three years later, he ordered the state to pay 1 million reais (US$540,000) compensation to the survivors for the wholly avoidable tragedy which had befallen their people. For the first time in 40 years, the Panará have hope.

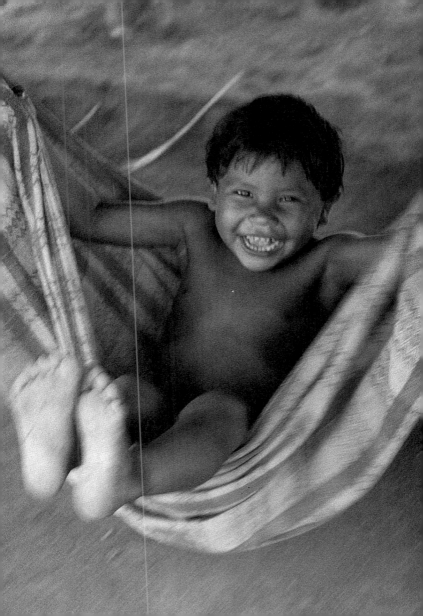

Road to ruin

THE NAMBIQUARA

The Nambiquara of western Brazil numbered up to 7,000 in 1915, but by 1975 only 530 of them remained. This tragic loss of life – more than 90% of the population lost in 60 years – was not brought about by any natural disaster, but by government projects, funded by the World Bank, and facilitated by FUNAI, the government Indian department.

In 1960, a highway was bulldozed through the fertile valley that was the Nambiquara's homeland. Although fully aware that this was Nambiquara land, FUNAI issued 'negative certificates' stating that there were no Indians in the area. Many Nambiquara died as a result

Anthropologist Claude Lévi-Strauss, who photographed the Nambiquara in the 1930s, described his pictures as creating 'a feeling of emptiness and sorrow… given the contrast between a past I had the joy of knowing and a present of which I receive heartbreaking accounts.' (1994)

of the sudden exposure to diseases such as flu and measles. As the road network spread, much of the lush valley was invaded by large companies and cleared for cattle pasture. The remaining Nambiquara were forcibly removed to a barren reserve.

The reserve was tiny, and completely inadequate – as many of the Nambiquara as could set off on the 200 mile walk back to their homelands. A FUNAI official who witnessed the catastrophe resigned in protest. 'When they reached the reserve site they were immediately struck by an epidemic of malaria and influenza, a result of the unhealthy conditions there. They realised they couldn't survive, and, utterly abandoned, they sought to return to their former villages. Almost 30% of the tribe died during the return home. It was a tragic march, with Indians dropping by the roadside.'

Thousands died on this terrible journey – one group of 400 Nambiquara lost all its children under the age of 15 to disease and hunger. Many of the others moved around the Sararé area for years, displaced, homeless and weakened by disease. Eventually a rescue operation was mounted, and the starving, wandering groups of Nambiquara were airlifted out. An International Red Cross team which visited in 1970 concluded that 'the condition of these Indians is a disgrace not only for Brazil, but for humanity as a whole.'

Yet little was left even for those Nambiquara who had escaped eviction or who eventually managed to return to their homeland. In the 1980s, the World Bank poured money into improving the highway, reducing the Indians' land still

'Nambiquara' is a Tupi Indian name, which means 'long ears' or 'ear hole', after the wooden plugs they wear in their ear lobes. The Pareci, neighbours of the Nambiquara, call them 'Uiakoakore' – 'those who sleep on the ground' – referring to their unusual custom of sleeping in the sand using the ashes of the fire to keep warm at night. Most Brazilian Indians sleep in hammocks.

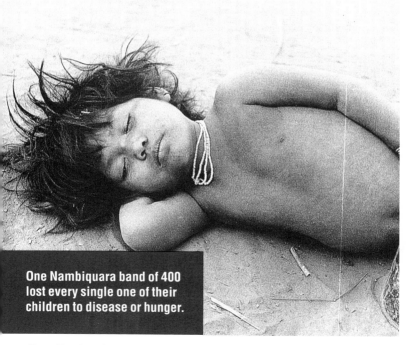

One Nambiquara band of 400 lost every single one of their children to disease or hunger.

further. Thousands more loggers, miners and settlers poured in. The Sararé area saw a massive influx of goldminers: in November 1996 some of the local Kithaurlu Nambiquara were brutally beaten up and tortured. Only after national and international protests did the police clear the area of 10,000 goldminers.

Today the Nambiquara face intimidation from loggers and other settlers, who are cutting down their wood, and hunting the game on which the Indians rely for survival. Many now feel that they must

In the 1980s, the World Bank funded a road which cut through Nambiquara land, bringing ranching, mining, logging – and disease – in its wake. The impact on the tribe was devastating.

defend their land themselves. One, José Nambiquara, explained to Survival, 'The whites still want to rob. But we are guarding our land. In 1991, we created a boundary so that the whites could see it and respect it. Manu was nearly killed by a bullet which cut his head open. We always go armed now. We warn them, "If you shoot, we will shoot too." But I have never killed a white.'

'All our ancestors lived together, Nambiquara, Irantxe, Pareci. Then came another wanting to rob us…. They came in hidden to touch us. Our land has been sold, stolen. The government doesn't say anything. I remain sad. Whites come to take our land so that we become 'civilised' and work like them to live.' Tamrã, an Irantxe leader, 1976

Genocide

In August 1993 a scrappy note arrived at the FUNAI office in the city of Boa Vista in the northern Amazon. Written by a missionary nun in the Yanomami village of Xidéia, it read 'The Indians [from near Haximú] are all here... they don't want to go back because the goldminers went to a *maloca* [communal house] nearby and killed seven children, five women and two men and destroyed the *maloca*.' It had taken a month for news of the killings to reach the outside.

The story had started several months earlier, when miners had killed other Yanomami whose relatives later retaliated, killing two miners. It was then that a group of heavily armed miners set out to 'teach a lesson' to the Yanomami community of Haximú on the Venezuela-Brazil border.

It took a long time for details to emerge. On arrival the miners had opened fire on the *maloca*, in which mainly women and children were at home, before moving in to burn it down. Those who could, fled for their lives, and a handful of survivors took refuge in the forest. An old and blind woman was left behind: the miners kicked her to death. A baby lying in a hammock survived the gunfire and was chopped up with a machete. After it was over and the miners had left, some survivors crept back and cremated the

A Yanomami survivor of the massacre at Haximú. She and other survivors cremated their dead, and carried the ashes in baskets through the forest for several days until they found refuge in a neighbouring Yanomami village.

On average, one tribe was wiped out every two years in the 20th century.

THE FIERCE PEOPLE

Portrayals of Indians as violent savages remain common. Perhaps the worst recent example is the image created of the Yanomami by the US anthropologist Napoleon Chagnon, whose studies are standard references in anthropology. Chagnon fabricated a sensationalist and racist image of the Yanomami, calling them 'sly, aggressive, and intimidating' and falsely claiming that they 'live in a state of chronic warfare'.

Chagnon's work has been severely criticised by others with extensive experience of the Yanomami and has undoubtedly been detrimental for the Indians. It was referred to by the Brazilian government when it planned to fragment Yanomami land in 1988, in a proposal which would have been catastrophic for the Indians and which was only prevented by a vigorous campaign. The UK government rejected a funding proposal for an education programme with the Yanomami in the 1990s, saying that any project with them should work on 'reducing violence'. The doyen of British anthropology, Sir Edmund Leach, relied on Chagnon when he opposed Survival helping the Yanomami in the 1970s, claiming they would then 'exterminate one another'. Survival rejected this advice and along with the Brazilian Pro-Yanomami Commission, CCPY, became instrumental in securing Yanomami land rights in 1992.

bodies, taking the ashes of their kin with them on their journey to the next village. The final total was 16 Yanomami dead.

After seemingly interminable delays, a case was eventually brought to court at the end of 1996 and a judge found five miners guilty of genocide. Although 19- to 20-year sentences were handed down, only two men actually ended up in prison, the others having fled.

This was Brazil's second conviction for genocide. The first, two years previously, was levied on a rubber tapper who was found guilty of the 'ultimate crime' following the murder of eight Oro Uim Indians – mostly children and women – in 1963. He organised an attack on the group, and after the massacre the survivors were taken to his plantation where they were enslaved. By the 1990s, the Oro Uim numbered only 55 individuals.

The Brazilian courts' recognition of these killings as genocide is an important acknowledgement of the seriousness of the crime. However, pointing the finger at a handful of miners and a rubber tapper could also be described as missing the point – if a few miners massacring 16 Yanomami is genocide, then to what extent is the Brazilian state's appalling treatment of Indians also genocidal?

In the Yanomami case, the Brazilian government must bear some of the responsibility: for over four years they

'This is my message: don't forget the Yanomami and other indigenous peoples of Brazil and the world. Our blood is flowing, we are hungry and we are ill. We can't continue like this. We tribal peoples need land to hunt and to fish and to live in peace – not to fight. We can't fight like you here – your forebears made bombs and these fell on Indians in Brazil. We are not protected. There is nowhere else to escape to, we are surrounded. The authorities only destroy more and more, they are using up the riches of the earth. I looked in a shop window today and I saw a lot of goods – glasses, shoes and clothes. You lack nothing, yet you want more and more. You have a lot of cars but Indians don't want cars, planes and electricity. We want land. The land gives food and health for us to live with a full belly. Without the land we have no food. I leave this message in your hearts.'

An appeal made by Davi Yanomami during a visit to Europe, 1999

'Genocide is not only killing off Indians with gunfire. Genocide is also injustice, collaborating with the aim that the Indian and his culture should disappear... We cannot in the name of development have contempt for the Indian, take his lands, massacre him. Absolutely not.'
Orlando Villas Bôas, 1971

failed to expel miners working illegally in the Yanomami area, allowing disease and violence to spread. As the mining invasion and heath crisis accelerated, the government actually threw out all health teams working with the tribe. The Yanomami population fell – through disease and attacks – by nearly one fifth in the space of seven years.

The Yanomami are not an isolated case, and many others are even more extreme: government policies of integration, settlement or development have been directly responsible for the demise of many Indian tribes. The deliberate state neglect of Indians (whether because of corruption, underfunding or political expediency) has destroyed many more. And sometimes there are policies which are openly racist, and even more clearly genocidal in effect – in 1999 one politician presented a bill calling for an amnesty for those miners who have committed crimes in indigenous or protected areas, and several are pressuring the government to open up all Indian areas to mining.

Faced with such a situation, many during the last 50 years predicted the impending demise of the entire Brazilian Indian population. This is no longer a danger: the Indian population is now increasing overall – but small, isolated tribes are still being put at risk, and their people killed.

Cinta Larga girl. In 1963 her tribe suffered one of the most vicious attacks ever inflicted on an Indian community.

Genocide is a crime against humanity and so becomes the responsibility of everyone.

The United Nations convention on genocide describes it as 'any of the following acts committed with intent to destroy, in whole or in part, a national, ethnical [sic], racial or religious groups, as such:

a) killing members of the group;

b) causing serious bodily or mental harm to members of the group;

c) deliberately inflicting on the group conditions of life calculated to bring about its physical destruction in whole or in part:...'

According to the UN, as well as genocide itself the 'punishable acts' include conspiracy, incitement, and the attempt to commit genocide; and complicity in genocide.

The facts, stated bluntly, are that the Brazilian state has pursued and is pursuing policies which lead inevitably and predictably to the destruction of vulnerable tribes. Although the state does not intend to destroy them, its 'development' projects do take over their land, which the government knows will destroy them. Even where there are no state projects, it still fails to protect tribal land from invasion. The result is genocide, and moreover one which is very easily avoided.

End of the line

THE AVÁ CANOEIRO

Only five hours drive from Brazil's capital, Brasilia, tiny groups of Indians have been hiding in the vast thorny scrub land. They are the Avá Canoeiro – the last remnants of a proud and strong tribe which has been on the run since 1780, and is now on the verge of extinction.

For hundreds of years they fiercely resisted the white intruders, who dispatched hit men to kill them. They travelled swiftly along the rivers in canoes, becoming known as 'canoeiros'. They tipped their arrows with metal and hurled heavy wooden clubs attached to ropes to fight off the attacks. Frequently they raided settlers' farms to steal cattle and horses for their meat. In 1811, the Portuguese prince regent proclaimed,

Left: Naquatcha.

Over: Her great nephew and niece, Trumak and Putdjawa, are the last of their people. Although still children, from time to time they ask, 'Who will we marry?'

'There is at present no alternative but to intimidate and if necessary destroy them.' By 1850, the Avá Canoeiro had placed the whole of north Goiás in central Brazil under siege.

But during the course of the 19th century the Portuguese Brazilians colonised the land and hunted down the Avá, and by the 1870s they were largely forgotten. Reduced in numbers, the remaining Avá Canoeiro spent decades in small bands of 10 or fewer, hidden in the scrub, forced to become nomads.

In the early 1980s, hundreds of construction workers moved in to build a hydroelectric dam on the Tocantins river, on Avá Canoeiro land. The dam's lake has drowned the Indians' last refuge and hunting grounds, the Serra de Mesa. As construction began, the government Indian department, FUNAI, commenced an urgent mission to contact remaining groups – it soon became clear that very

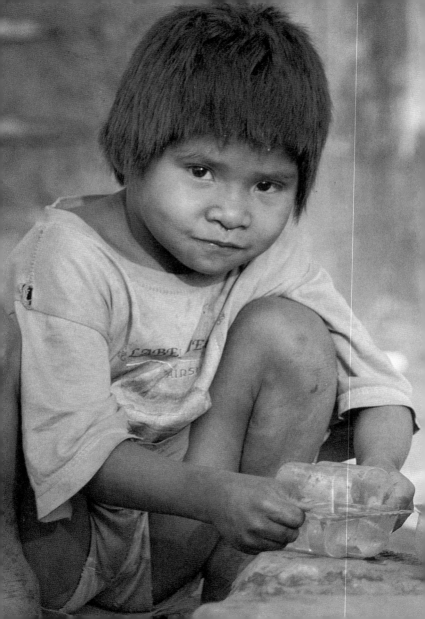

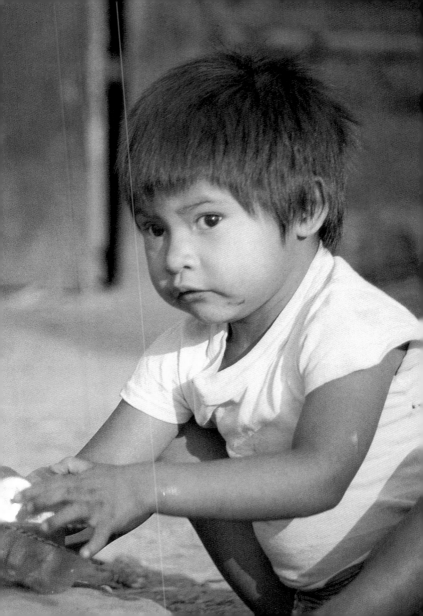

few Avá Canoeiro were left. In 1983, FUNAI eventually contacted an Avá Canoeiro couple, Iawi and Tuia, and Tuia's mother and aunt, Matcha and Naquatcha. The tiny group had survived a vicious massacre in 1962, and had then spent 20 years hiding in caves high up in the mountains. At night they would come down to raid settlers' gardens for food. Otherwise they had to survive off small mammals like rats and bats. Tuia terminated her pregnancies, so that the group could move quickly and silently.

Another small group of Avá Canoeiro, which numbers around a dozen people, had been contacted in Tocantins in 1973.

Nearly all were scarred from the bullets of gunmen hired by the Camagua ranch, owned by a Brazilian bank. The group was found living hidden in a marsh – their last refuge on what had been their hunting ground, now cut up by barbed wire fences – and they were suffering from malnutrition. FUNAI moved them to the Araguaia national park on Bananal Island, 250 miles away. Nobody knows for certain if there are any more Avá Canoeiro.

Since they made contact with FUNAI, Iawi and Tuia have had two children, Trumak and Putdjawa. If they do not meet up with other members of their tribe, the great Avá Canoeiro nation will probably become extinct.

The Serra de Mesa dam flooded much of the Avá Canoeiro's land, drowning their last refuge and hunting grounds.

PLANTS

Brazil, and particularly the Amazon, is a hugely varied environment, and its indigenous peoples have a tremendous knowledge of the natural world. Different parts of hundreds of plants are used not only for food, medicine, and building houses and canoes, but also for weaving baskets, hammocks and slings, for making blowguns, poisons, bows and arrows, for body paints and ritual purposes, and even for soap, deodorants, contraceptives and perfume.

The Yanomami use 500 species of plant for food, medicine, making objects and building houses. The Ka'apor use 112 different plant species for medicinal purposes alone.

Amazonian plants have given the world quinine and curare, now used in medicines throughout the world.

Nothing
to live for

THE GUARANI

For as long as they can remember, the Guarani have been searching – searching for a place revealed to them by their ancestors where people live free from pain and suffering. They call it the 'Land without Evil', and they are still seeking it. The plight of their tribe today makes it more necessary than ever.

The Guarani have been in intense contact with outsiders for hundreds of years, but have retained their own very separate identity – and with it their 'constant desire to seek new lands, in which they imagine they will find immortality and perpetual ease' (Pero de Magalhães de Gandavo, 1576). Over hundreds of years, the Guarani have travelled vast distances in search of such lands, and Guarani communities can

now be found scattered far from their homelands in the south, across five Brazilian states. At the beginning of the 19th century, for instance, hundreds of Indians set off on a journey, inspired by Guarani seers foretelling the end of the world and prophesying that an escape from doom could be found in the Land without Evil. They marched 500 miles from the south of Mato Grosso do Sul almost as far as São Paulo. Here they were met by a Brazilian army expedition, which suffered severe losses in the ensuing battle and was forced to allow them to settle there.

This permanent quest is indicative of the unique character of the Guarani, a 'difference' about them which has often been noted by outsiders. Today, this manifests itself in a more tragic way: profoundly affected by the loss of almost all their land in the last century, the Guarani suffer a wave of suicide unequalled in South America.

A bereaved Guarani mother and her children waiting beside a coffin. The wave of suicides that has struck the Guarani in the last 15 years is unequalled in South America.

TOBACCO

Tobacco is traditionally an important plant for many Brazilian tribes. Different peoples consume it in different ways: leaves may be sucked, boiled into a paste and eaten, dried and ground into snuff, or smoked in a pipe or cigar. Some tribes use a hollow bone to blow snuff up their own or others' noses. Some, like the Yanomami, often keep a wad of tobacco in the lower part of their mouths. As well as using it as a relaxing drug, many tribes view it with reverence and use it in rituals and for healing. Among the Araweté, although everyone smokes tobacco, only the shamans inhale. Shamans often blow tobacco smoke over the sick, sometimes as a cure, and sometimes as protection from the effects of evil forces.

Once 1.5 million Guarani occupied a homeland of forests and plains totalling some 135,000 square miles in four South American countries. Today those in Brazil number just 30,000 – still the largest tribe in Brazil – and are squeezed onto tiny patches of land surrounded by cattle ranches and vast fields of soya and sugar cane. As Paulito, an elderly Guarani shaman, explains, 'I always remember one old man said, "The whites – they're going to finish us off. They're going to finish off our houses, finish our fish, even our crops. And once all our forest is gone, we as a people will be finished. It's all going to change and our land will become very small." And you know, that man, all those years ago, calculated absolutely right.'

In the 15 years to 2000, over 300 Guarani killed themselves, mostly

Araweté shaman

Some Guarani communities, tired of waiting for the authorities to restore their land, have returned on their own. This is often dangerous as the ranchers employ hit men to keep them off the land.

children and young adults. The youngest was Luciane Ortiz, aged just nine. For such a profoundly spiritual people, the theft and destruction of their land has been overwhelming. Rosalino Ortiz puts it this way, 'The Guarani are committing suicide because we have no land. We don't have space any more. In the old days, we were free, now we are no longer free. So our young people look around them and think there is nothing left and wonder how they can live. They

> **'We Indians don't want money or riches. We want enough land to live on how we like.'**

sit down and think, they forget, they lose themselves and then commit suicide.' Amilton Lopes says, 'Suicides occur among young people because they are nostalgic for the past. Young people are nostalgic for the beautiful forests, they want to eat fruits from the forest, they want to go out and find honey, they want to use natural remedies from the forest. In Dourados where there have been most suicides a young person told me he didn't want to live anymore because there was no reason to carry on living – there is no hunting, no fishing, and the water is polluted.'

Squeezed onto tiny patches of land, living in cramped and polluted communities, suffering an epidemic of suicide and violence, it is perhaps only the deeply spiritual side to the Guarani's nature that has enabled them to survive at all. At great risk to themselves some villages have successfully re-occupied land that was once theirs, seizing it back from the farmers who now claim it as their own. A Guarani woman, Marta Silva, declared, 'I think of the conditions in which we live – abject poverty, those little houses. We have nothing to eat and yet our people still sing with such joy, with such hope, always in search of the Land without Evil… We Indians don't want money or riches. Do you know what we want? We just want enough land to live on how we like.'

A lorry passes a makeshift Guarani camp. Many Guarani who have been forced off their land survive by selling handicrafts on the roadside.

26 Guarani children under the age of 14 have poisoned, hanged or shot themselves since 1992:

Luciane Ortiz, aged 9; Agnaldo da Silva, aged 14; Hélio Marques aged 14; Fortunata Escobar aged 10; Hélio Marques aged 14; Janeva Rosa aged 13; Luciana Espínola aged 15; Marina Vasques aged 14; Nena Aguero aged 12; Nilsa Isnarde aged 13; Ovídio Ramires aged 13; Roasana Isnarde aged 13; Marcenei de Souza aged 11; Alceu Raulino aged 13; Idele Isnarde aged 13; Nilza Cavanha aged 13; Valdecir A. Vieira aged ; Franciso Duarte aged 13; Alexandrino Quevedo aged 1; Oswaldo Martins aged 12; Valdir Vieira aged 12; Vanildo Vilhalva aged 2; Pedro da Silva Pedro aged ; da Silva aged 13; Valdir aged 1; Aparecida Pereira da aged 1; da Oliveira aged ; A aged 1; e P e a o a 1; u a

Year by year breakdown of the 304 recorded Guarani suicides from 1986-1999.

Source: CIMI-Mato Grosso do Sul

56 people: there was more than one suicide per week in 1995

29 people

23 people

8 people

5 people

1986 1987 1988 1989 1990 1991 1992 1993 1994 1995 1996 1997 1998 1999

'These Indians are vagabonds, they are the pariahs of society.'

Ezequiel dos Santos, owner of an alcohol distillery, refering to the Guarani, 1990.

Shamanism

The word 'shaman' is thought to originate with the Evenk tribe of Siberia, but today is used to refer to those people anywhere in the world who are specialised in communicating with the natural world and its spirits. They are generally healers, using both natural medicines and a belief in the spirit world in their cures. Shamans may represent the spirits to the people on earth, and they are respected for their powers.

All tribal peoples in Brazil have – or at least had – individuals who act as shamans. Of course, different peoples have their own names for shamans, and they take different roles in the community. Some, such as the Guarani

A Yanomami shaman healing a feverish child. The process is exhausting for the healer and can last several hours, during which time a close bond is established between the shaman and his patient. The strong sense of security that this creates is fundamental to all Yanomami healing.

karais, are seers and have the gift of prophecy; some are eloquent singers and poets; others are regarded as tricksters or entertainers. The Tukano believe shamans can turn into jaguars, the most powerful and feared animal in the forest. Among some peoples, only men can become shamans, in others, women also. Some peoples believe you must be born into the tradition, while the Araweté, for instance, believe everyone has the quality or the ability to be a shaman. For the Waiãpi, you can have this quality, but you can also lose it.

Shamans use dance, chant, and mind-altering plants to enter trances and communicate with spirits. Most interpret dreams and the meanings of daily events, and are experts in the mythic cycles of their people. Becoming a shaman can require years of demanding apprenticeship, often involving dietary and sexual restrictions.

'We Yanomami learn with the great *shapiri* [spirits]. We learn how to know the *shapiri*, how to see them and listen to them. Only those who know the *shapiri* can see them, because the *shapiri* are very small and bright like lights. There are many, many *shapiri* – not just a few, but lots, thousands like stars. They are beautiful and decorated with parrot feathers and painted with *urucum* [red berry paste]. Others have earrings and use black dye and they dance very beautifully and sing differently. The whites think that when we Indians do shamanism we are singing. But we are not singing, we are accompanying the music and the songs. There are different songs: the song of the macaw, of the parrot, of the tapir, of the tortoise, of the eagle, of all the birds which sing differently. So that's what the *shapiri* are like. They are difficult to see.

'Whoever is a shaman has to accept them, to know them. You have to leave everything: you can't eat food or drink water, you can't be near women or the smell of burning, or children playing or making a noise – because the *shapiri* want to live in silence. They are other people and they live differently. Some live in the sky, some underground, and others live in the mountains which are covered with forests and flowers. Some live in the rivers, in the sea and others in the stars, or in the moon and the sun. Omame [the creator] chose them because they were good for working – not in the gardens, but for working in shamanism, for curing people. They are beautiful but difficult to see. The *shapiri* look after everything. The *shapiri* are looking after the world.'

Davi Yanomami, shaman in his village, Watoriki-Theri ('people of the windy mountain').

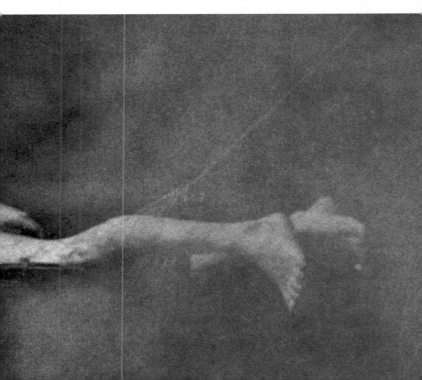

YANOMAMI DRAWINGS OF SHAMANIC SPIRITS

TOOTHACHE (top)

'These are the spirit dogs of 'Kamakari'. This spirit sends his hunting dogs to catch the victim's teeth. The dogs pull out the essence of the teeth and bring them to Kamakari who eats them. That's what Kamakari does, he eats teeth, and he's always hungry. Luckily, he lives far away and you can't see him; but if he does get your teeth and eat them, it's very, very painful.'

COURAGE (bottom)

'The jaguar is the spirit of strength and courage. People who are brave have this spirit inside them, it lives inside their chests. The shaman can summon the spirit to people who are weak and ill, it gives them strength to fight their sickness. It can even save them from too early a death.'

Drawings by Joseca Yanomami.

HALLUCINOGENS

Like many peoples, Brazilian Indians use plants to alter their mental state, to enter the world of spirits and religion. Tribes in the north of the country take a hallucinogenic snuff called *yopo* or *yakoana*. They roast the inner bark of certain trees, mix the ash with powdered leaves and blow it into their nostrils with a hollow cane.

Other tribes make a drink called *caapi* (also called *ayahuasca*) by boiling particular species of creepers and vines. This is taken during special festivals where the Indians re-enact their mythology, and seek support from good forces and protection from malevolent ones. Amazonian Indian designs, such as paintings on houses, are influenced by the visions.

Tribes in northwest Amazonia grow and use *ipadú*, or *coca*. The leaves are roasted, pounded and mixed with ash. The resulting fine green powder is placed in the mouth where the active ingredients (including cocaine) slowly induce a stimulating effect.

All such plants are themselves considered to be powerful and sacred, and potentially dangerous if mistreated. They are only used in ritual contexts under strict conditions, and never casually or for entertainment.

Against all odds

THE WAIÃPI

The Waiãpi of the north Amazon were nearly wiped out by invasions of their land in the 1970s; today they are recovering and trying to ensure their survival as a people – but in their struggle to do so they have faced fierce hostility and discrimination from powerful interests, missionaries and government agencies.

The Waiãpi tell of a past when they lived in the south, along the banks of a huge river. Aggressive missionary and slave raiding incursions during the colonial period forced them to flee far from this first homeland and settle in the rainforests of the north Amazon. Here they saw few white men – only the occasional hunter or mineral prospector – until a road was bulldozed through

The Waiãpi have pulled themselves back from the very brink of extinction over the last 30 years, and now their population is growing.

their land in 1975-6. Exposed to diseases to which they had no immunity, large numbers died, including almost all of their elders. Their population, estimated at 6,000 in 1824, plunged to only 150 as miners swept through their rainforest home, contaminating and destroying it.

Joapirea Waiãpi was orphaned and adopted by one of the arriving miners. He later returned to the Waiãpi, rejecting the 'suffering' in the city. 'The first time we met the miners, my father and mother died of diseases caught from them... A lot of Waiãpi died. The Waiãpi died of flu and measles. People were suffering. They had sore tongues, they were

Two thirds of Brazil's tribal peoples live in the Amazon.

'In the future I do not want my grandchildren to say that their grandfather was crazy. I do not want them to say I gave our land away to the Brazilians. What I want the future generations to say is that I defended our lands well. If the Brazilians settle here we will have nothing to eat. The game will disappear, the Brazilians will kill it all. Then in the future there will be no more Waiãpi. But I will not know it. I will not be alive.' Wai Wai, a Waiãpi leader

vomiting, so the Waiãpi began to run away. The miners didn't care. They wanted to finish off the Waiãpi. The miners just kept on arriving... We didn't know about medicine in those days. The miners did, but they didn't want to give any to the Indians.'

As the miners flooded in, the few Waiãpi survivors, speaking no Portuguese and with little understanding of what was happening to them, fled deeper into the forest. Slowly they began to recover from the shock of first contact, which had so very nearly destroyed them.

The Waiãpi have now mapped out their territory, marking boundaries and building new settlements, strategically sited to protect themselves. In recent years they also began small-scale gold panning in the areas already cleared by white miners. This provided a small income which they used to buy cloth, salt and sugar in local towns. But in 1997, the white miners, their crony politicians, fundamentalist missionaries of the New Tribes Mission, and even the local Indian affairs official – all angry

that the Indians themselves might get an income from their own land – tried to ban the Waiãpi from panning, and called for their territory to be reduced. The government paralysed their health and education projects by refusing to allow doctors and teachers in. The Waiãpi felt surrounded by enemies: 'They are all the same – federal agents, gold miners, trappers, timber workers... they all answer to the same boss.'

Survival and the Indigenous Advocacy Centre (CTI) mounted a vigorous international campaign and in 1999, a judge ruled that the Waiãpi did have the right to surface mine on their land. During years of suffering, the Waiãpi have defended themselves against all attacks – whether physical or not – and once more their population is growing. They have shown that it is possible for a small and isolated tribe to survive and assert itself successfully.

Feasts and dances are important to the Waiãpi, and celebrate events in the natural cycle such as fish spawning.

'Our cries go out to the four corners of the country, not to demand health and community projects – this is secondary in the present drama being lived out by the Indian peoples of Brazil. What is more important at the moment is the guarantee of our lands, our heritage and the cradle of our cultural traditions.'
Assembly of Indian Representatives, 1978

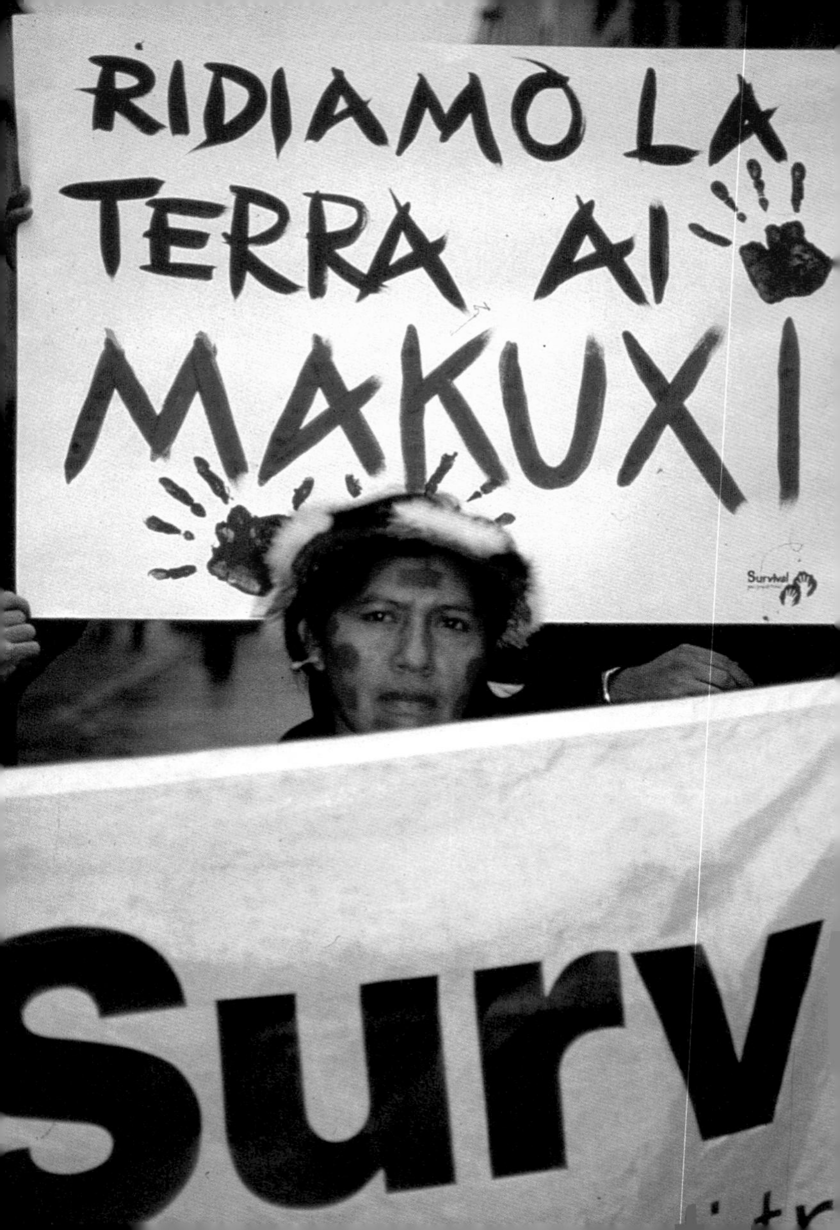
RIDIAMO LA
TERRA AI
MAKUXI
Survival
Surv

Land ownership

Under international law tribal peoples own the lands they live on and use. This has been the case since the 1957 convention (no. 107) of the United Nations' International Labour Organisation, a law which Brazil signed up to as long ago as 1965. In spite of this, Brazil remains the only country in South America (apart from tiny Suriname) where Indians are deemed to have no ownership rights whatsoever over their own lands. This is both a violation of Brazil's legal responsibilities and contrary to UN thinking of the last 40 years or more, and it places all Indian land there in an extraordinarily vulnerable position.

'Give back the land to the Makuxi.' The Makuxi have suffered at the hands of police and gunmen during their struggle for land rights. Umbelina Viriato and other Makuxi representatives travelled to Europe in 1995 to bring their story to the international media. Their struggle for land rights and Survival's campaign with them continue.

In Brazil, Indians are legally minors and their communities can own no land at all – they can simply live on and use certain areas of government-owned land which have been recognised as 'Indian areas' or 'parks'. This recognition, usually by presidential decree, can easily be modified or annulled by subsequent presidential decisions: all too often this is exactly what happens.

For land to be set aside for Indian 'use', it must first be 'delimited' (its boundaries outlined on a map) and then 'demarcated' (physical markers set up on the ground). These steps usually take years to carry out and are never even begun without vigorous pressure from those individuals within government (and outside) who are real Indian supporters. The process invariably comes up against powerful lobbies of Indian opponents, often miners or loggers, or local politicians who are

'This land that the whites call Brazil belonged to the Indians. You invaded and took possession of it. The Indians who are the true owners of this land, have no rights to a piece of it... The Indian was the first inhabitant of this land. We didn't invade anybody's land in other countries. We just want the land that was ours, which belongs to us.' Megaron Txukharramae, 1981

seeking votes or a share of their profits, or both. Most senior army officers have also proved staunchly opposed to Indian land near the country's borders – as well as having seized control of the government in Brazil's recent past, they still want a firm hand over what they see as strategically sensitive areas.

The effect of all this is that there is constant pressure on the government not to create new Indian areas, to reduce the size of existing ones, and actually to annul those already demarcated. In 1996, the minister of justice introduced a decree giving third parties such as loggers or settlers the right to challenge the limits of demarcations. Eight areas were to be 'revised' – in other words, reduced. Cases such as these can drag on unresolved for many years.

The same minister signed an act to reduce the demarcated land of the 12,000 Indians living in Raposa/Serra do Sol – he wanted the Indians to live in a few small enclaves, as was proposed in other cases, whilst freeing up at least a fifth of their land for mining and ranching. After lengthy protests, the president promised to recognise the whole territory as one area. Even then a group of ranchers who were occupying

Indian land, supported by local politicians, went to court in an attempt to overturn this decision.

Such reductions of Indian land are invariably presented as being 'in the national interest' – yet they are motivated rather by the economic interests of a few powerful individuals. Certainly they are disastrous for the Indian peoples concerned and of little or no benefit to the Brazilian population as a whole.

The only effective answer to the constant attempts to reduce Indian land, and to begin to redress the violent injustices which Indians in Brazil have faced for five centuries, would be for Brazil to stop breaking international law and begin to recognise Indian ownership rights over their lands. Ownership offers the only long-term security for tribal peoples anywhere. Land must be owned by the whole people or community, the title must be inalienable and given in perpetuity. Anything less than this, for example giving plots to individuals, or granting titles that can be transferred or sold, is guaranteed to ensure the eventual breakup of the land, as people can be bullied, bribed or deceived into giving up their plots. Giving individual

CLEONICE'S STORY

The Makuxi, Wapixana, Ingarikó and Taurepang peoples live in the northern Amazon, and face some of the worst violence against Indians anywhere in Brazil as they struggle to have their land, Raposa/Serra do Sol, legally recognised. Over a dozen Indians have been killed, and hundreds more have been beaten up and had their homes and livestock destroyed by the local police and by ranchers and settlers who oppose the Indians' campaign.

Maria Cleonice Servino, a young Wapixana woman, describes a typical incident when military police, called in by the local rancher, attacked her village in 1987:

'I was three months pregnant at the time. Twelve trucks full of police rolled up. They went about breaking everything and hitting people. They broke the ribs of one of my brothers, and threw women down onto the ground – their children were crying and hiding under the tables. I remained standing, so a soldier came up to me and ordered me to lie down. I said I would not. "I am not a dog that you can order about. I am in my home." By now it was raining and all the children were covered in mud. They threw a table at some of the men and people were thrown on top of each other. Everyone was crying except for me – I don't know why.

'The soldier hit me in the stomach with the butt of his gun. "Why don't you kill me? I am three months pregnant and if my baby dies it will be your fault. You may be the boss in the barracks, but the bosses here are us." I tried to push the gun away with my hand and he said, "You've escaped this time, but you won't next time."'

'I want to talk of *urihi*. *Urihi* for us means 'our place', 'our land'. This *urihi* Yanomami is not for sale. *Urihi* has no price at all. There is no money that can pay for the Yanomami land. The Yanomami already looked after this earth long before any politicians arrived. Our communities don't have paper. Our 'paper' is our thoughts, our beliefs. Our 'paper' is very ancient: we had it long before the white people arrived and wanted to take our *urihi*. Our thought is different to yours. We only cut down a bit of forest, to work, to plant. We do not cut down trees to sell. We cut with the permission of the community. We plant food to sustain the community. Omame [the creator] gave *urihi* to the communities for them to live here. That's where we Indians were born. We want our *urihi* to be respected. Whites brought disease into *urihi* and contaminated us, our blood, our lives. We already have natural food, so there is no need to destroy the forest and plant again. We need the trees and fruits and streams and mountains full of wind, and rain and birds singing. We need all of this – alive.

The earth is like a father because he looks for food. Water is like a mother – when you are thirsty she gives you water. *Urihi* is like a brother, a true brother, which gives energy for us to grow, for our children to grow, alongside trees and animals and fish. Rain falls to cool the earth. It cleans us. We have roots. Demarcation of our land means roots – they are buried there in our earth. Our roots are very old but never dead – for this reason we have forest and good earth and minerals, which is what the white people want, but we won't let them. Remember us – you have force. You are the only ones with strength outside. Authorities criticise you for helping us, but you are not afraid. Continue to pressurise, and so let the Yanomami live.'

Davi Yanomami to Survival supporters, 1992

titles has in fact been used by governments in the USA and Chile as a deliberate ploy to destroy Indian communities.

Though nothing of course can fully guarantee the future of any people, such land ownership is the best possible protection that Indians in Brazil can achieve. It will not, of itself, prevent all invaders trying to enter their land, or killing them, and it will not stop the spread of contagious diseases which have already taken hold – but it will give Indians the strongest legal tool to protect their own lands and lives. Of course, policing and health care will still be required. But securing Indian land is a crucial first step, and could be done for very little money, certainly no more than is currently used for demarcation. Existing Indian areas could easily be redesignated as land owned by the tribe, and where new areas are needed, the international funds already available for demarcating Indian lands could be used to fund the required mapping.

Yet the expected hostility against this proposal is such that even many Indian supporters within Brazil fear that, if it is raised, it will provoke an even harder anti-Indian movement. But the fact that what is normal in other Amazonian countries is still considered taboo in Brazil is surely part of the problem: Indians stand no chance of ever owning their land unless the debate about this is launched inside Brazil.

The anti-Indian lobby in Brazil rests on those who seek their own profit from exploiting Indian land, and is fuelled by the deep-seated and pervasive racism which sees tribal people as inferior to 'whites'. This lobby will oppose a call to Indian land ownership and will declare this to be another plot or fantasy of the 'enemies of Brazil'. These arguments are of course wholly spurious: many Indian supporters (and, for that matter, many supporters of Survival International) are Brazilian and some are in the senior ranks of the government or church. Most of these quietly support the justice of Indian land ownership – but in the country as a whole there is an ingrained racism which ensures that the matter is never openly raised.

Brazil's illegal refusal to acknowledge Indian ownership rights is one of the longest-running gross human rights violations in the world today. It is a scandal which leads to incalculable suffering. It is time for the Brazilian government to act, to stop breaking the law, to accept that the few Indian peoples who have survived the last 500 years own their land. Such a move would be the single most effective step finally to stop the genocide of the most vulnerable of Brazil's Indians, and give them a real chance of survival.

WRITE TO THE PRESIDENT OF BRAZIL

If you would like to help the tribal peoples in Brazil then you can do so by writing a polite letter to the president of Brazil, stating that you oppose the continual onslaught on the lands of Brazil's Indians. Your letter can be very brief – please write in Portuguese, English, or your own language.

The Brazilian authorities are sensitive to international public opinion about Indian peoples – your voice really does count.

Presidente da República
Palácio do Planalto
Praça dos Três Poderes
70150-900, Brasília DF
Brazil

(Begin your letter 'Your Excellency')

Take action

After 500 years, Brazil's tribal peoples should finally have their rights respected – their rights to life, to peace and safety, and to own their own land. You can help – by sending £10 to Survival's urgent appeal.

The Indians who told us their stories for this book are not looking for sympathy, but they do feel cheated and disinherited – and many are extremely vulnerable. What they need is for people around the world to join them in their protest and so help ensure that their rights are respected. The best way you can do this is through Survival – for over 30 years, Survival has been working with tribal peoples and successfully mobilising public support to pressure governments, as well as companies, into respecting tribal peoples' rights and protecting their land. We are unique in our field – and we need your help. If you care about what you have read, and can spare £10, an envelope, a stamp and 2 minutes, then please do send us a donation. There are so many more urgent cases in Brazil, and with your help we can take them on.

Even better, you can give more regularly to Survival's work with tribal peoples in Brazil and worldwide by using the banker's order form overleaf. A regular gift cuts down on administration and helps us to plan our work more effectively – even £2 a month would be a great boost to our work.

Please help – you really can make a difference to the future and survival of the some of the world's most threatened peoples.

THANK YOU.

I WANT TO HELP TRIBAL PEOPLES

Forename	Last name

Address

Postcode	Country

Email

Banker's order form (UK only)

You can cancel a banker's order at any time by notifying us and your bank/building society.

Bank/building society name

Bank/building society address

Postcode

Please pay Survival *(tick chosen amount or fill in amount)*:

£20	other £	**each year**	Account no.
£6	other £	**each quarter**	Sort code
£2	other £	**each month**	Signature
Starting on			Date

and/or I wish to make a gift of:

£100	£50	£25	**£10**	other £

*Please make cheques payable to '**Survival**'.*

Survival accepts credit card donations in any currency online by secure method at **www.survival-international.org/card.htm** or by phone **++44 (0)20 7242 1441**

I am a UK taxpayer, and want Survival to reclaim the tax on this donation and any I make from now on *(tick box)**:

	Date

Please return this form to:
Survival, Freepost NWW3155A, Liverpool L69 1GH, United Kingdom
No postage required if posted in UK. Do not return to your bank/building society.

*You must pay an amount of income or capital gains tax at least equal to the tax we claim on your donation (currently 28p for every £1 you give). For official use: To The Cooperative Bank, 62-64 Southampton Row, London WC1B 4AR (08-90-61) Survival International Charitable Trust a/c 65022641, quoting the customer's name and our reference. Survival will not pass on any of your details to any other organisation.

Survival

SURVIVAL IS A WORLDWIDE
ORGANISATION SUPPORTING TRIBAL
PEOPLES. IT STANDS FOR THEIR RIGHT
TO DECIDE THEIR OWN FUTURE AND
HELPS THEM PROTECT THEIR LIVES,
LANDS, AND HUMAN RIGHTS.

Today there are one hundred and fifty million tribal people worldwide. Almost all are persecuted relentlessly – they are flooded by dams, wiped out by disease, driven from their homes by logging and mining, and evicted by settlers.

Survival was founded in 1969 in response to the atrocities inflicted on Indians in Brazil. For more than thirty years it has worked to safeguard the rights of tribal peoples all over the world – from Siberia to the Kalahari – and to help them solve their own problems: problems which come from outsiders wanting their land and what is in it.

Survival campaigns for tribal peoples' right to own their lands and to live how they choose; it supports their own organisations, and offers them a platform to put their case to the world; its educational work opposes racism and shows that tribal peoples are far from primitive – in the long term this is the most effective force for change.

Survival does not accept money from any national government. Its supporters around the world finance everything it does and give Survival its powerful and independent voice.

Survival
for tribal peoples

www.survival-international.org

ACKNOWLEDGEMENTS

Many Indians and their organisations have shared their views with Survival over three decades and welcomed us into their communities. This book has been inspired by them. They are too numerous to mention but we are extremely grateful to them all. Survival would also like to thank the many other individuals and organisations in Brazil and elsewhere who have shared their views and information over the years. We thank all those photographers who generously donated photos.

Thanks also to Zé Karajá da Cunha, Clare Dixon, John Hemming, Telma Holanda, Lesley Anne Knight and Jan Smith for their help and encouragement in producing this book.

CAFOD is the member for England and Wales of Caritas International, a worldwide network of Catholic relief and development organisations. It believes that all human beings have a right to dignity and respect and that the world's resources are a gift to be shared by all men and women, whatever their nationality, race or religion. Information on CAFOD's work in Brazil and elsewhere can be found at http://www.cafod.org.uk

Survival is grateful for the encouragement and help given by CAFOD in producing this publication.

BRAZILIAN ORGANISATIONS

A directory of Indian organisations in Brazil is published and distributed free of charge by MARI - the Indigenous Education Unit at the University of São Paulo (grupioni@usp.br). Non-governmental organisations working with Indians in Brazil can be contacted via the following websites or email addresses:

ANAI National Indian Support Association: anai@lognet.com.br
CCPY Pro-Yanomami Commission: www.uol.com.br/yanomami
CIMI Indigenous Missionary Council: www.cimi.org.br
CPI Pro-Indian Commission, São Paulo: cpisp@uol.com.br
CTI Indigenous Advocacy Centre: cti@dialdata.com.br
ISA Socio-environmental Institute: www.socioambiental.org
OPAN Operation Native Amazon: opan@ax.apc.org

PHOTO CREDITS

Cover: Kayabi girl © CIMI; inside cover: Yanomami shaman © Claudia Andujar; following page: Enawene Nawe father and son © Fiona Watson/Survival; contents: Arara man © John Miles/Panos; introduction: © Eduardo Viveiros de Castro; p2 © Charles Vincent/Survival; p3 © Adrian Cowell/Hutchison Picture Library; p4 © Fernando López/CIMI-Norte 1; p5 © Jan Smith; p8 © José Idoyaga/Survival; p11 and 12 © Royal Geographical Society Picture Library; p14 © Sue Cunningham/SCP; p16 © Philippe Erikson; p20 © Erling Söderström/Survival; p22 © Erling Söderström/Survival; p23 © Philippe Erikson; p24 © Fiona Watson/Survival; p26 © Fiona Watson/Survival; p28 © Fiona Watson/Survival; p30 © Fiona Watson/Survival; p31 © Fiona Watson/Survival; p32 © Pedro Martinelli; p35 ©Pedro Martinelli; p36 ©Pedro Martinelli; p38 ©Pedro Martinelli; p41 © Pilly Cowell/Hutchison Picture Library; p42 © Pilly Cowell/Hutchison Picture Library; p44 © Claude Lévi-Strauss; p46 © Claude Lévi-Strauss; p47 ©Marcos Santilli/Panos Pictures; p48 © Carlo Zacquini/CCPY; p50 © Sue Cunningham/SCP; p51 © Helen Dent/Survival; p52 © CIMI/Survival; p54 © Fiona Watson/Survival; p56 © Adrian Cowell/Hutchison Picture Library; p58 © Adrian Cowell/Hutchison Picture Library; p59 © Victor Englebert 1980/Survival; p60 ©João Rippper; p62: Araweté shaman © Eduardo Viveiros de Castro; p63 ©João Ripper; p64 © Simon Rawles; p67 ©João Ripper; p68 © Victor Englebert 1980/Survival; p70: Yanomami © Claudia Andujar; p73 © Victor Englebert 1980/Survival; p74 © Fiona Watson/Survival; p76 © Alan Campbell/Survival; p77 © Dominique Gallois/Survival; p78 © Mario Ruggari/Survival; p81 © Fiona Watson/Survival; p82: Yanomami © Peter Frey/Survival; p83 © Fiona Watson/Survival; p85: Yanomami © Alfredo Cedeño/Panos Pictures; p86 © Survival; p91: Kayapó © Sue Cunningham/Survival; back cover: Arara girls © John Miles/Panos Pictures.

Map p6: © 1993 Digital Wisdom, Inc.